BLAZERS

U.S. MILITARY ASSAULT VEHICLES

by Carol Shank

CONTENT CONSULTANT:
MAJOR (RET.) MARGARET GRIFFIN, MS
U.S. ARMY
ATLANTA, GEORGIA

READING CONSULTANT:
BARBARA J. FOX
READING SPECIALIST
PROFESSOR EMERITA
NORTH CAROLINA STATE UNIVERSITY

Blazers is published by Capstone Press,
1710 Roe Crest Drive, North Mankato, Minnesota 56003.
www.capstonepub.com

Library of Congress Cataloging-in-Publication Data
Shank, Carol.
    U.S. military assault vehicles / by Carol Shank.
    p. cm. — (Capstone blazers: U.S. military technology)
    Summary: Describes the assault vehicles used by the U.S. military.
    Includes index.
    Audience: Grades 4-6.
    ISBN 978-1-4296-8613-6 (library binding)
    ISBN 978-1-62065-209-1 (ebook PDF)
1. Armored vehicles, Military—United States—Juvenile literature. 2. Amphibious assault ships—
United States—Juvenile literature. 3. Airplanes, Military—United States—Juvenile literature.
I. Title.
UG446.5.S44 2013
623.74—dc23   2012003751

Editorial Credits

Brenda Haugen, editor; Kyle Grenz, designer; Laura Manthe, production specialist

Photo Credits

Photo courtesy of General Dynamics Bath Iron Works, 18-19; Photo courtesy of General
Dynamics Electric Boat, 17; South Carolina National Guard photo by Sgt. Roberto Di Giovine,
cover (Top); U.S. Air Force photo by Master Sgt. William Greer, 24-25, Staff Sgt. Brian Ferguson,
28-29, Staff Sgt. M. Erick Reynolds, 26-27, Staff Sgt. Shane A. Cuomo, 9; U.S. Army photo by
Pvt. DeAngelo Wells, 14-15, Staff Sgt. Sadie Bleistein, 21; U.S. Marine Corps photo by Lance Cpl.
Orlando Perez, cover (Bottom), Cpl. Brain J. Slaght, 4-5, Cpl. Christopher R. Rye, 13 (Top), Cpl.
Cory Yenter, 13 (Bottom), Cpl. Jason D. Mills, 6-7, Gunnery Sgt. Scott Dunn, 10-11; U.S. Navy
photo by MC2 Michael Russell, 22

Artistic Effects

deviantart.com/Salwiak, backgrounds

Printed in the United States of America in
Stevens Point, Wisconsin.
032012   006678WZF12

TABLE OF CONTENTS

CALL TO ACTION

WARNING

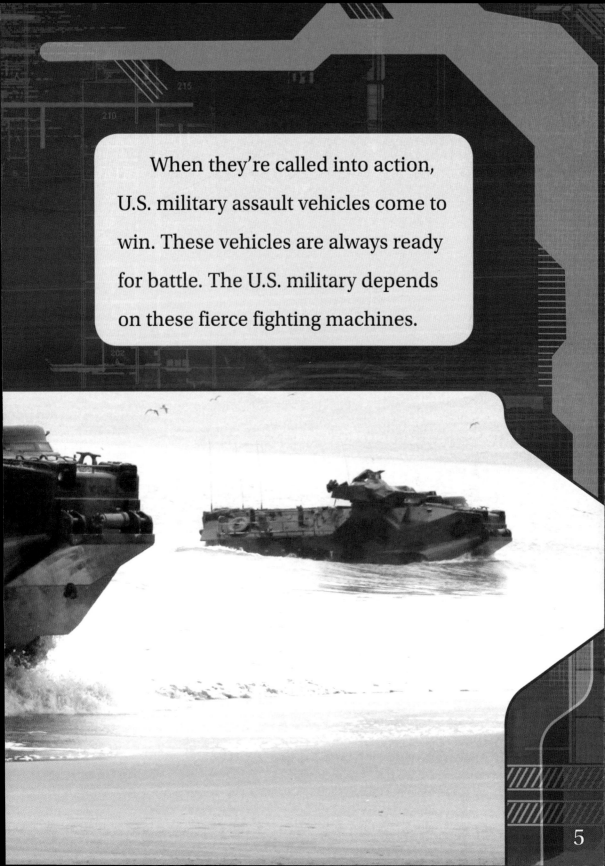

When they're called into action, U.S. military assault vehicles come to win. These vehicles are always ready for battle. The U.S. military depends on these fierce fighting machines.

CHAPTER 1

TRACKED VEHICLES ON THE ATTACK

The M1A1 Abrams tank has thick armor. Its cannon blasts enemy tanks. The M1A1 rarely misses its target and even finds targets in the dark.

 The Abrams tank is nicknamed "The Beast" because of its power.

The M2A2 Bradley Fighting Vehicle crosses all types of land. It carries troops and protects them with its powerful guns. When not moving, it launches TOW **missiles** at enemy tanks.

missile—an explosive weapon that can travel long distances

 Wires attached to TOW missiles send signals to soldiers to help guide the weapons.

Navy ships carry AAV-7s near beaches to fight enemies. These **amphibious** assault vehicles leave a ship and travel through water to the shore. An AAV-7 carries 25 Marines.

AAV-7

amphibious—able to work on land or in the water

 **FACT** AAVs helped the Marines capture two important bridges during Operation Iraqi Freedom in 2003.

CHAPTER 2

WHEELS MOVE OUT

Helicopters carry the Marines' interim fast attack vehicles (IFAVs) to battlefields. IFAVs climb steep hills. They are fast too. IFAVs travel up to 96 miles (154 kilometers) per hour.

The U.S. Army's Strykers have light armor and eight wheels. Most carry soldiers, but some **transport** cannons and other big weapons.

transport—to move or carry something or someone from one place to another

**FACT**

A Stryker's tires have hard small tires inside. If all eight tires go flat, the small tires let the Stryker keep moving.

CHAPTER 3

ASSAULT BY SEA

Virginia-class attack submarines prowl underwater. They fire missiles at land targets and **torpedoes** at enemy ships and submarines.

torpedo—an underwater missile

masts

FACT The crew sees the water's surface with the help of two masts that act like cameras.

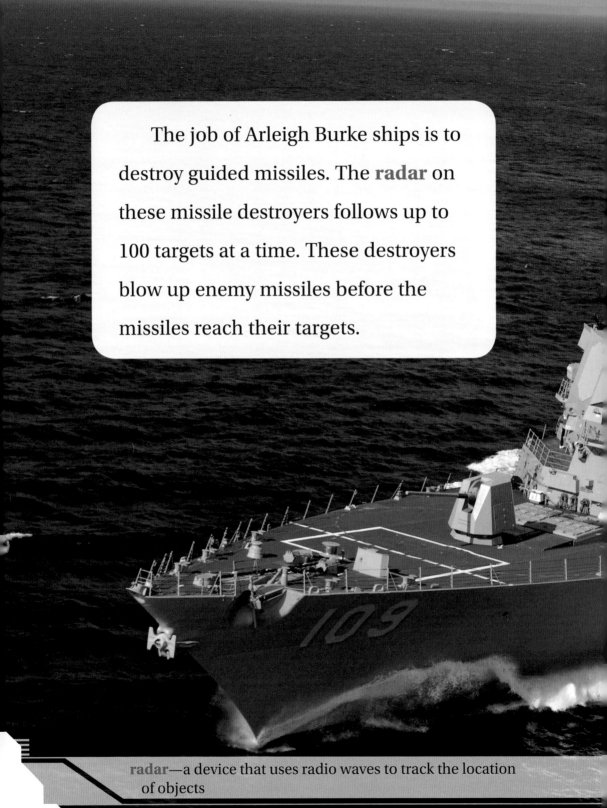

The job of Arleigh Burke ships is to destroy guided missiles. The **radar** on these missile destroyers follows up to 100 targets at a time. These destroyers blow up enemy missiles before the missiles reach their targets.

radar—a device that uses radio waves to track the location of objects

 Destroyers have rounded sides that hide them from enemy radar.

CHAPTER 4

POWER IN THE SKY

The AH-64 Apache is an attack helicopter. The pilot locks onto enemy targets and launches missiles. The AH-64 Apache also blows up enemy missiles.

 **FACT** Apaches are tough. They carry out missions during the day or night and in any kind of weather.

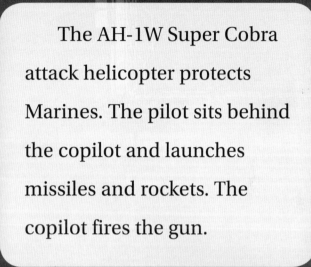

The AH-1W Super Cobra attack helicopter protects Marines. The pilot sits behind the copilot and launches missiles and rockets. The copilot fires the gun.

FACT Cobras were important helicopters in the Vietnam War (1959–1975). They flew very low to the ground and used their weapons to protect soldiers.

The Navy's F/A-18 Hornet and Super Hornet rocket through the air at nearly 1,200 miles (1,931 km) per hour. Their main jobs are striking enemy planes and bombing ground targets.

F/A-18
Super Hornet

FACT On the first day of the Gulf War (1991), two Hornets dropped 16,000 pounds (7,257 kilograms) of bombs.

The B-2 Spirit **stealth** bomber flies to its targets unseen by enemy radar. It unloads bombs on heavily guarded enemy targets.

FACT The B-2 Spirit's engines are inside its wings. This design hides the bomber from enemy **sensors** that would find the engines' heat.

stealth—the ability to move without being detected

sensor—an instrument that can detect changes and
send the information to a controlling device

Future assault vehicles will be even more powerful. They will have more fire power, travel faster, and hide from enemies better.

MQ-9A Reaper unmanned vehicle

In the future, unmanned vehicles will do more of the fighting, keeping soldiers safe.

GLOSSARY

amphibious (am-FI-bee-uhs)—able to work on land or in the water

missile (MISS-uhl)—an explosive weapon that can travel long distances

radar (RAY-dar)—a device that uses radio waves to track the location of objects

sensor (SEN-sur)—an instrument that can detect changes and send the information to a controlling device

stealth (STELTH)—the ability to move without being detected

transport (transs-PORT)—to move or carry something or someone from one place to another

torpedo (tor-PEE-doh)—an underwater missile

READ MORE

Alpert, Barbara. *U.S. Military Fighter Planes.* U.S. Military Technology. North Mankato, Minn.: Capstone Press, 2013.

Doman, Mary Kate. *Big Military Machines.* All about Big Machines. Berkeley Heights, N.J.: Enslow Elementary, 2012.

Winchester, Jim. *Jet Fighters: Inside & Out.* Weapons of War. New York: Rosen Pub., 2012.

INTERNET SITES

FactHound offers a safe, fun way to find Internet sites related to this book. All of the sites on FactHound have been researched by our staff.

Here's all you do:

Visit *www.facthound.com*

Type in this code: 9781429686136

Super-cool stuff! Check out projects, games and lots more at
www.capstonekids.com

INDEX